37

MiG-21

Titles in the *Super Profile* series:

Avro Vulcan (F436)
B29 Superfortress (F339)
Boeing 707 (F356)
de Havilland Mosquito (F422)
Harrier (F357)
Mikoyan-Gurevich MiG 21 (F439)
P-51 Mustang (F423)
Phantom II (F376)
Sea King (F377)
SEPECAT Jaguar (F438)
Super Etendard (F378)
Tiger Moth (F421)
Bell UH-1 Iroquois (F437)

Further titles in this series will be published at regular intervals. For information on new titles please contact your bookseller or write to the publisher.

ISBN 0 85429 439 2

A FOULIS Aircraft Book

First published 1984

Published by:
Haynes Publishing Group
Sparkford,
Yeovil,
Somerset BA22 7JJ

Distributed in USA by:
Haynes Publications Inc.
861 Lawrence Drive,
Newbury Park,
California 91320, USA

Produced by:
Winchmore Publishing Services Limited,
40 Triton Square,
London NW1 3HG

Chant, Christopher
Mig 21 super profile. — (Super profile)
1. MIG (Fighter planes)
I. Title II. Series
523.74'63 UG1242.F5

ISBN 0-85429-439-2

Picture Research: Jonathan Moore

Printed in Yugoslavia

Contents

Genesis

The best Soviet fighter of the early 1950s was the Mikoyan-Gurevich MiG-15bis, a remarkable achievement for the Soviet aircraft industry, and a devastating shock to the Americans in the skies over war-torn Korea during late 1950 and early 1951. The Americans prevailed over the MiG-15 series with the excellent North American F-86 Sabre, but it was clear that much of this dominance was achieved by US pilot training and the superior equipment of the American fighters. While the MiG-15 had a definite performance edge over the F-86 in certain important parameters such as climb and turn rates, it was also found, however, to possess several adverse characteristics such as a tendency to stall and spin in very tight turns, pronounced snaking at Mach numbers in excess of 0.88, and poor handling at high angles of attack.

Improved aircraft were already under flight test during the Korean War – namely the MiG-17 and MiG-19 from the same design stable – but the lessons of air combat during the Korean War also showed the need for a new generation of interceptor fighters with high superonic performance. The lessons were there for all to see, the Americans responding with the remarkable Lockheed F-104 Starfigher, a Mach 2 'manned missile' (or, rather, manned missile-launch platform) in which all was sacrificed to speed and rate of climb. The Soviet interpretation of the same lessons produced a radically different requirement, issued in the autumn of 1953. The new fighter was required for short-range interception and was to have design provision for the later installation of the air-interception radar for limited all-weather operations. High performance was stipulated, especially in speed, climb rate and rate of turn, but range was to be a secondary consideration. The primary armament was to consist of air-to-air missiles, though a secondary armament of powerful cannon was required for the combined air-to-air and air-to-surface roles, in which latter capacity the new fighter was also to carry a light bombload.

The approach to the requirement of the OKB (experimental design bureau) of Artem Ivanovich Mikoyan and Mikhail Iosifovich Gurevich (an acronym of whose names forms the abbreviation MiG by which the

Seen in Pakistani markings, the MiG-15UTI was the trainer version of MiG's first truly successful jet fighter, and the first of a highly important series.

Above: Seen in the form of a Chinese-built Shenyang F-6 in the markings of the Pakistani air force, the Mikoyan-Gurevich MiG-19 was the logical development of the MiG-15 via the MiG-17, offering supersonic performance on two relatively small turbo-jets as a result of its light weight and excellent aerodynamic qualities.

Below: A development of the MiG-15, the Mikoyan-Gurevich MiG-17 offered better handling, performance also being improved by the adoption of a more sharply swept wing and other aerodynamic improvements. This is a North Korean aircraft.

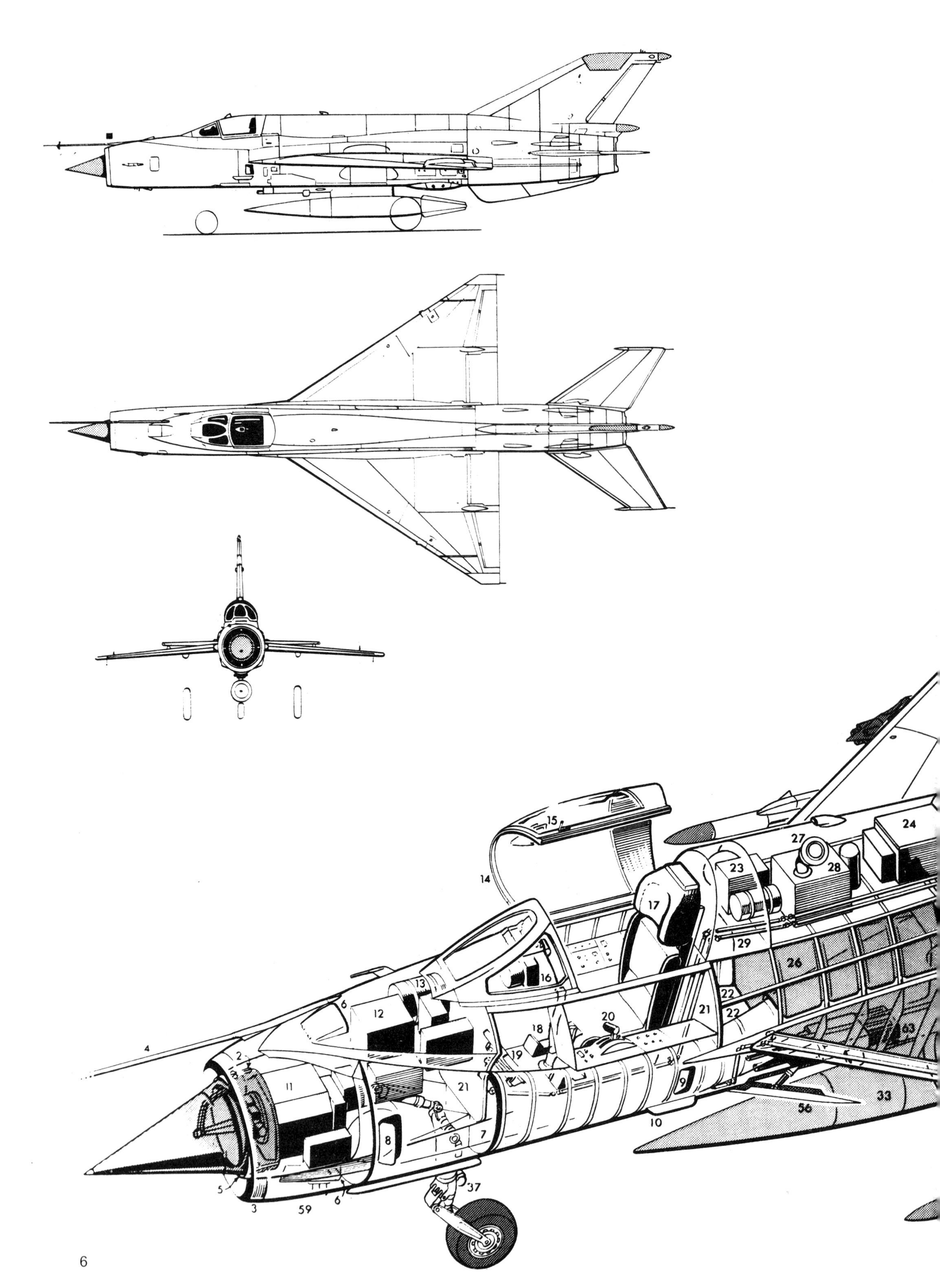
15
14
24
27
23
28
17
29
26
16
13
12
6
22
22
21
20
18
63
4
2
19
11
21
9
33
56
10
8
7
5
37
3
59
6

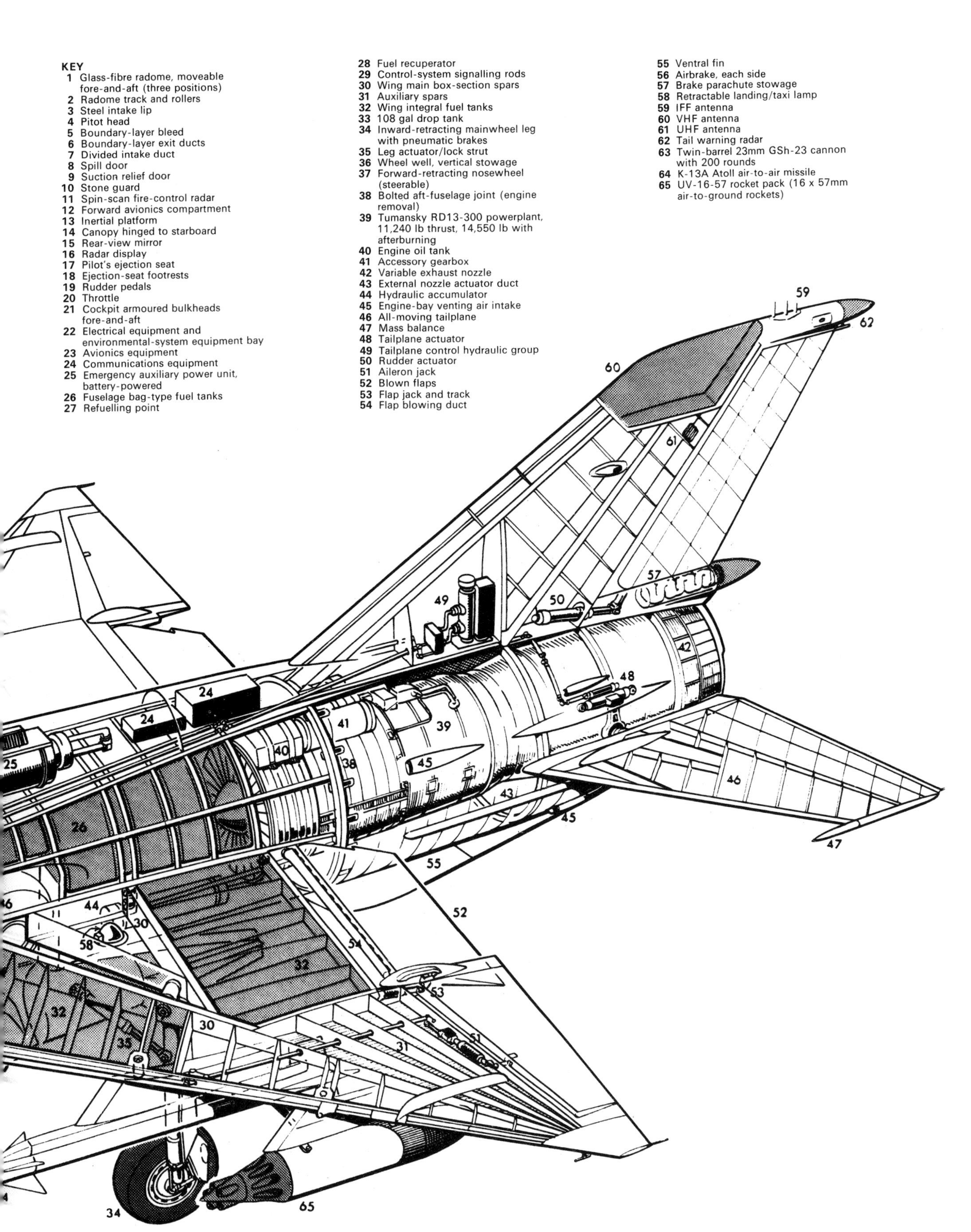

KEY
1 Glass-fibre radome, moveable fore-and-aft (three positions)
2 Radome track and rollers
3 Steel intake lip
4 Pitot head
5 Boundary-layer bleed
6 Boundary-layer exit ducts
7 Divided intake duct
8 Spill door
9 Suction relief door
10 Stone guard
11 Spin-scan fire-control radar
12 Forward avionics compartment
13 Inertial platform
14 Canopy hinged to starboard
15 Rear-view mirror
16 Radar display
17 Pilot's ejection seat
18 Ejection-seat footrests
19 Rudder pedals
20 Throttle
21 Cockpit armoured bulkheads fore-and-aft
22 Electrical equipment and environmental-system equipment bay
23 Avionics equipment
24 Communications equipment
25 Emergency auxiliary power unit, battery-powered
26 Fuselage bag-type fuel tanks
27 Refuelling point
28 Fuel recuperator
29 Control-system signalling rods
30 Wing main box-section spars
31 Auxiliary spars
32 Wing integral fuel tanks
33 108 gal drop tank
34 Inward-retracting mainwheel leg with pneumatic brakes
35 Leg actuator/lock strut
36 Wheel well, vertical stowage
37 Forward-retracting nosewheel (steerable)
38 Bolted aft-fuselage joint (engine removal)
39 Tumansky RD13-300 powerplant, 11,240 lb thrust, 14,550 lb with afterburning
40 Engine oil tank
41 Accessory gearbox
42 Variable exhaust nozzle
43 External nozzle actuator duct
44 Hydraulic accumulator
45 Engine-bay venting air intake
46 All-moving tailplane
47 Mass balance
48 Tailplane actuator
49 Tailplane control hydraulic group
50 Rudder actuator
51 Aileron jack
52 Blown flaps
53 Flap jack and track
54 Flap blowing duct
55 Ventral fin
56 Airbrake, each side
57 Brake parachute stowage
58 Retractable landing/taxi lamp
59 IFF antenna
60 VHF antenna
61 UHF antenna
62 Tail warning radar
63 Twin-barrel 23mm GSh-23 cannon with 200 rounds
64 K-13A Atoll air-to-air missile
65 UV-16-57 rocket pack (16 x 57mm air-to-ground rockets)

Compared with the MiG-17, the MiG-19 had an extra 10° of leading-edge sweep, which gave it much the same angle as the MiG-21.

OKB is commonly known) was a logical development of the concepts embodied in the MiG-15 and its successors, tempered by two key factors. These latter were the initial decision to use the new Tumansky R-11 afterburning turbojet, and the aerodynamic researches carried out by the TsAGI (Central Aerodynamic and Hydrodrynamic Institute). At the time of MiG's decision to use the R-11 for the aircraft that emerged as the Mikoyan-Gurevich MiG-21, this neat single-shaft twin-spool turbojet had probably run only on the test-bench, and was qualified for service in 1956 at an initial dry rating of 8,598-lb (3,900-kg) thrust and an afterburning rating of 11,243-lb (5,100-kg) thrust. The association of Tumansky with the MiG bureau was already of long standing, for Sergei Konstaninovich had during World War II been the deputy of A. A. Mikulin, whose inline piston engines were used in most MiG aircraft of the period. After the war Tumansky was responsible for the design of the first Soviet axial-flow turbojet, the AM-5 redesignated RD-9 after the political disgrace of Mikulin in 1956, whereupon Tumansky became head of his erstwhile superior's engine design bureau. The RD-9 was used to very considerable effect in the MiG-19 supersonic fighter, reaffirming MiG's connection with Tumansky after initial reliance upon the centrifugal-flow RD-45 (licence-built Rolls-Royce Nene) in the MiG-15 series and upon the VK-1 (Klimov-derived development of the RD-45) in the MiG-17. The MiG OKB had been impressed with the early maturity of the AM-5/RD-9 series in the MiG-19, the engine being notable for its slimness and good power-to-weight ratio. The MiG OKB therefore had every reason to expect much of the R-11, which emerged as an extremely compact engine with most of the accessories located on the underside of the compressor, an overhung first rotor stage (one of the first such applications) without the normal inlet guide vanes, a very trim annular combustion chamber, and a multi-flap variable nozzle for the large afterburner. For its time, the R-11 was a singularly advanced engine, but applications of the engine in aircraft such as the MiG-21, Sukhoi Su-15 and Yakovlev Yak-28 at first suffered from considerable delays as the complex teething problems of the engine were corrected and useful thrust rating became available.

The input of the TsAGI was more fundamental, being con-

Above: The MiG-19 also saw the removal of the tailplane from the previous fin-mounted position to the fuselage.

Below: Three-view of the MiG-21SMT 'Fishbed-K', with additional side views of the MiG-21UM 'Mongol-B' (bottom left) and MiG-21F 'Fishbed-C' (bottom right).

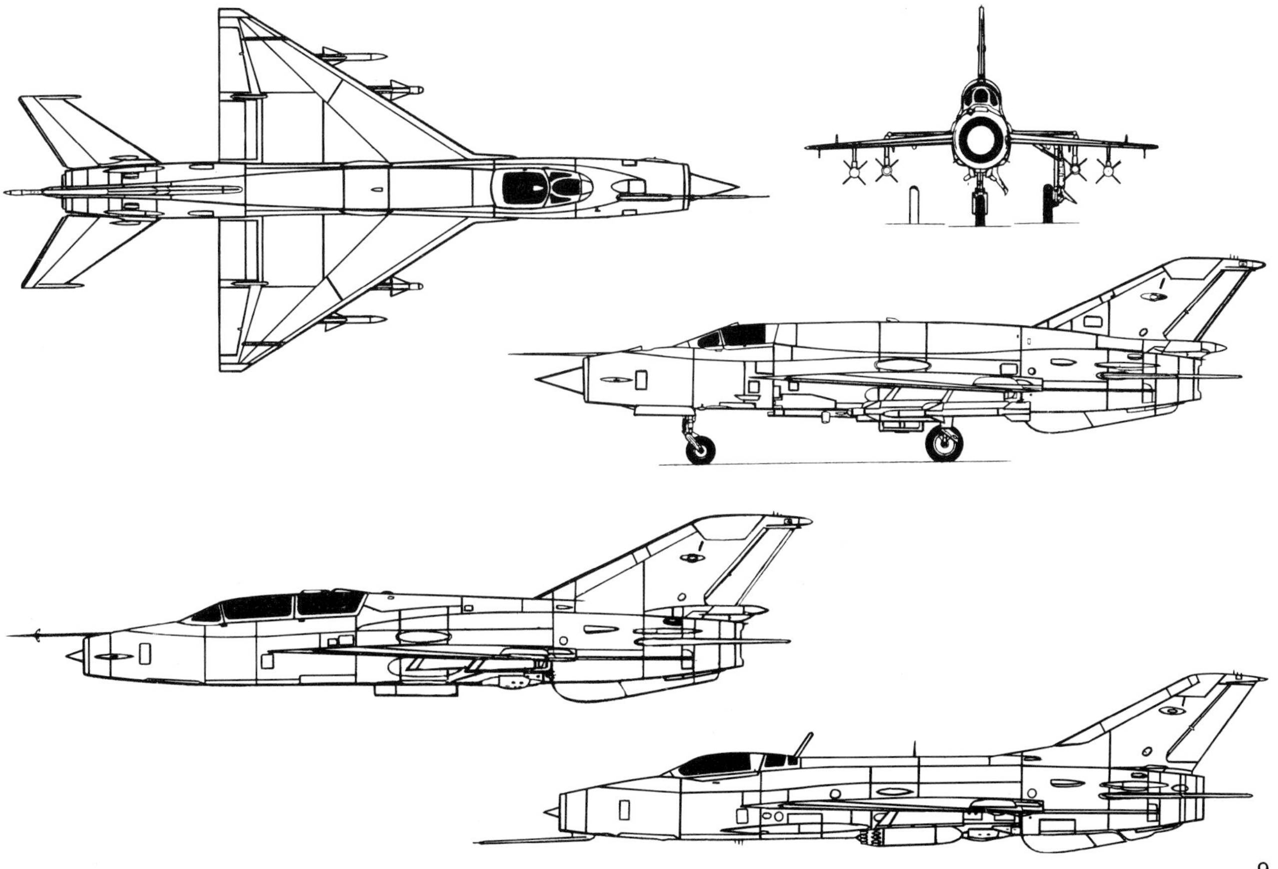

The MiG-19 was a truly remarkable aerodynamic achievement, particularly in the design of the wings' great sweep and high aspect ratio. The wings were also structurally very stiff.

cerned with the advanced aerodynamic factors that conditioned the basic airframe. For some years the TsAGI had been conducting theoretical and wind-tunnel research into the optimum configuration for aircraft designed to reach Mach 2, and had finalized its ideas into two basic layouts. Each of these basic shapes used a long slim fuselage with slab tailplanes and mid/low-set swept wings, though one basic concept called for tapered wings with a leading-edge sweep of 55° while the other dictated a delta wing with a leading-edge sweep of 57°. Given the nature of the Soviet aircraft industry, which promotes the development of prototypes in considerable numbers regardless of cost (leading finally to a production programme that works best when major modifications are well spaced, allowing the major production of variants to keep down unit costs), the MiG OKB could move ahead rapidly with the construction of prototypes conforming to both TsAGI configurations.

The first of these prototypes was the E-50, probably completed quite rapidly as it used a wing based on that of the MiG-19, which conformed in essence to the TsAGI taper-wing configuration. This aircraft was completed in the middle of 1955, before a flight-cleared R-11 was available. The aircraft was thus fitted with an 8,377-lb (3,800-kg) afterburning thrust RD-9E and an S-155 rocket at the base of the vertical tail. The prototype weighed in at a maximum of 18,739 lb (8,500 kg), and armament of two NR-30 30-mm cannon was fitted. Exact dates are not available (a fact that bedevils much of Soviet aviation history, at least from the Western standpoint), but it appears that the E-50 was first flown in November 1955, the pilot being V. P. Vasin. The basic success of the MiG design concept was rapidly validated, for the E-50 returned a maximum speed of Mach 2.3, making it undoubtedly the fastest non-American aircraft in the world with the exception of the Fairey FD.2, a pure research aircraft. However, the E-50 was only a prototype despite its armament, and the combination of turbojet and rocket was not intended as anything but an expedient to produce the required thrust for test purposes.

Overall design responsibility for this important project was exercised by Mikoyan himself, though his health was not of the best, and much responsibility was shouldered by Mikoyan's deputy, Rotislav A. Belyakov, who assumed complete charge of the MiG-21 programme in 1964 and of the MiG OKB on Mikoyan's death in 1970. Gurevich retired in the early 1960s and died in 1976, so Belyakov must be regarded as one of the chief architects of the MiG-21 design, being notable particularly for the development of high-speed swept wings.

By the end of its design development, the MiG-21 had developed into the markedly different MiG-21bis (seen here in Finnish markings) with a totally revised airframe, different engine and enhanced capability.

Despite the performance success of the E-50, the MiG OKB had higher regard for the two tailed deltas under construction with the designations E-4 and E-5. That this is the case is indicated by the fact that the pilot assigned to these two types was the OKB's chief test pilot, G. A. Sedov. A fourth prototype was under construction with the designation E-2, this being the definitive tapered-wing prototype, for which the test pilot was V. A. Nefedov. The first of the tailed deltas to fly was the E-4, which took to the air in December 1955. No flight-cleared R-11s were yet available so, like the E-50, the E-4 had to make do with the less powerful RD-9E. The first flight of the E-4 was of considerable historical importance, for this Sedov-piloted aircraft can be regarded as the first true prototype of the MiG-21 series despite its different engine.

The overall importance of the programme was now of national proportions, and a separate but interrelated experimental laboratory was established under the leadership of A. V. Minaev to tackle the host of aerodynamic, system and structural problems thrown up by the development of the MiG-21. Just as importantly, the Minaev organization was tasked with the development of the aircraft in relation to the industrial programme that would be involved in the mass production of the type. Thus the research organization was largely responsible for turning the hand-built prototype vehicle into the production-line service model.

The R-11 engine finally became available to the MiG OKB in the spring of 1956, and prototypes with this engine were soon ready for flight trials: the taper-wing model was the E-2A and the delta-wing model the E-5. The E-2A was first flown by Nefedov in about May 1956, the E-5 following in the hands of Sedov on 16 June 1956. Considerable aerodynamic refinement had gone into these revised prototypes, one of the more noticeable being the use of three fences on each wing to control the spanwise distribution of pressure. Both aircraft were revealed to the West in the 1956 Aviation Day flypast held at Tushino airfield outside Moscow on 24 June: the E-2A was then allocated the NATO Air Standards Co-ordinating Committee reporting name 'Faceplate', and the pure-delta E-5 the reporting name 'Fishbed'. Oddly enough, it was then believed for several years in the West that the 'Fishbed' was a research type that had not entered production, while the 'Faceplate', which had clear similarities to the in-service MiG-19, was believed to be in large-scale production for service with the V-VS (Soviet air force).

During 1965 the E-2A and E-5 were subjected to a thorough competitive evaluation, whose results were something of a surprise for the MiG OKB when

Above: This MiG-21UM 'Mongol-B' conversion trainer has only two underwing hardpoints but is fitted with flap-blowing.

Below: The MiG-21bis has a two-axis instrumentation boom and a neatly installed GSh-23 lower-fuselage cannon fitting.

Right and below right: Though blurred as a result of being taken through the canopy, these photographs are of considerable interest and show the left side and centre of a MiG-21PF's cockpit.

the E-5 failed to demonstrate a considerable superiority over the E-2A, especially in speed. Here the E-5 had been expected to excel, and part of the failure was traced to the spillage of air from the nose inlet. Once this deficiency had been cured, the E-5 perked up considerably in performance, and was soon recorded at 1,243 mph (2,000 km/h) in comparison with the 1,205 mph (1,940 km/h) of the E-2A. The competitive evaluation drew to a close in December 1956, and the E-5 was selected for production. The deciding factors seem to have been the lower wave drag and structural lightness of the delta wing used on the E-5, which were thought to combine with better supersonic manoeuvrability to promise a better interceptor. The advantages of the E-2A's wing configuration were assessed as better load-carrying capability at subsonic speeds but, as the type was then envisaged as a single-role interceptor, this factor was deemed secondary. It is interesting to speculate, given the MiG-21's future development as a multi-role fighter, what might have been developed had the Soviets opted for the taper-wing configuration of the E-2A.

With the E-5 selected for production, the designation MiG-21 was allocated. But before the large-scale production of series fighters could be contemplated, there remained a number of serious problems and shortcomings to be solved and eradicated. The MiG OKB therefore built an E-6 pre-production prototype for the solution of the engine and control problems. This aircraft was externally identical with the subsequent MiG-21 'Fishbed-B' pre-production model except that it had six wing fences.

The MiG-21bis is the definitive dual-role development of the basic aircraft, and has a completely revised structure for long life.

Another notable feature was the reuction of internal armament compared to that of the E-2A and E-5: these aircraft had featured an armament of three NR-30 30-mm cannon (mounted under the fuselage in line with the cockpit, with two guns to starboard and one to port), but the E-6 adopted a balanced armament of two 30-mm NR-30 weapons, one on each side of the lower fuselage. From this may be inferred that the addition of operational equipment was adding a measure of weight that was eroding performance. The trouble lay with the R-11 engine, which was as yet an immature powerplant of relatively low power: basic performance of the clean aircraft was indeed good, but this was bestowed as much by the excellent aerodynamics of the aircraft as by sheer engine power. Thus the addition of any extra weight had to be compensated by a reduction in performance, and an immediate way to reduce weight was the reduction of internal firepower. It nevertheless remained formidable, Soviet cannon of any particular calibre firing a heavier projectile with greater muzzle velocity than their Western counterparts of the same calibre.

Work on the E-6 was the responsibility of I. I. Rotchik, and the pilot assigned to the aircraft was Nefedov. Considerable progress towards engine reliability and handling harmonization was made, but the aircraft was lost after only eight flights. The E-6 suffered a complete engine failure at about Mach 2, and as Nefedov was bringing the aircraft down for a dead-stick landing he lost control and crashed on touchdown, subsequently dying from his injuries. The cause was traced to a mismatch of the engine and its inlet, resulting in a compressor stall. Nefedov was unable to relight the R-11 because the starter fuel tank was too hot and contained only vapour. And too slow a switch to emergency electrical power for tailplane actuation as the engine-powered hydraulic system failed near the ground meant that the pilot lost control. The matching of the inlet and engine was a relatively simple task, and was entrusted to the engineer Kokkinaki. Propulsion efficiency and reliability was much improved by the adoption of a translating inlet centrebody with three positions, and the provision of suction-relief doors under the leading edges of the wing roots.

The auxiliary power system presented greater problems, and while the engineer Burov called for a thorough-going revision of the electrical back-up system, Mikoyan decided to eliminate it altogether in favour of duplex hydraulics with a great (though not complete) degree of redundancy. This solution had been suggested by Belyakov.

Thereafter progress was rapid, particularly after the problems associated with control had been taken over by Mossolov, who proved that skill and insight could achieve what had previously eluded other designers. Various improvements and modifications were built into, or added to, a pre-production MiG-21 'Fishbed-B' aircraft, which underwent NII V-VS (Air Force Scientific Test Institute) trials during late 1957 and 1958, and in the latter year was finally cleared for production.

First-generation fighter

Though accorded the service designation MiG-21, the small number of aircraft derived from the E-6 were in reality pre-production machines used for the NII V-VS trials and for service evaluation in general. Compared with the E-6, the MiG-21 featured a single ventral fin in place of the earlier arrangement of two outward-canted fins; one instead of three wing fences; two underwing hardpoints for a primary armament of two K-13A (AA-2 'Atoll') IR-homing air-to-air missiles, or for a secondary armament of two UV-16-57 rocket pods (each with 16 2.24-in/57-mm unguided rockets) or other ground-attack loads; and provision for a gun armament of two 30-mm cannon, though the port weapon was usually omitted for weight-saving reasons.

That the MiG-21 was still in the very early stages of its service life is indicated by the fact that the R-11 engine had a life of only 100 hours, and by the fact that the pilot had to keep a careful eye on an interlinked airspeed and altitude instrument for instructions as to the moment he should change the tailplane actuation gear ratio. There was also an autostabilization system, working only on the pitch-and-roll axes and fitted with a q-feel unit.

The airframe was fundamentally a one-piece fuselage of basically circular section, tapering forward of the wing roots to a circular inlet with the translating centre-body already mentioned. Aft of the inlet area was the cockpit, the pilot being seated under a single-piece canopy with an integral windscreen. This canopy was hinged at the front, and connected with the ejector seat by gimballed mountings to leave the aircraft with the seat, so providing the pilot with protection from slip-stream blast. The R-11 engine was mounted in the centre of the fuselage on rails that slid to the rear for engine overhaul and change. The mechanical control rods for the rudder and tailplane ran through a small dorsal fairing to the input power units for the 10.39-sq ft (0.965-m^2) rudder and 47.9-sq ft (4.45-m^2) tail-plane, the halves of the latter each having an anti-flutter weight at its tip. The centreline ventral fin was flanked to port by a housing for the braking parachute and had an airbrake just forward of it, and under the fuselage in line with the wing root leading edges were a pair of small air-brakes. There was no wing centre section, the port and starboard wing panels being attached directly to frames on each side of the fuselage. The wings were each based on a single main spar at 33.33 per cent chord, there also being three auxiliary spars indexed at 90° to the fuselage centreline. The control and high-lift devices on the wings were simple, the former consisting of two fully-powered ailerons outboard (each with a small fence ahead of it), and the latter of two 10.06-sq ft (0.935-m^2) Fowler flaps inboard. These

Photographed in June 1962, this MiG-21F reveals the original production standard with undernose boom and simple airframe.

Above: Well displayed on this Finnish MiG-21F are the tailed delta configuration, Fowler flaps, twin hardpoints, all-moving tailplane and provision for two 30-mm cannon (one fitted) under the forward edge of the wing roots. Note the anti-flutter masses projecting forward of the tailplane tips.

Below: The MiG-21F had a forward-hinged one-piece canopy, and a single ventral fin with brake parachute stowed on its port side.

Right and below: Compared with later models of the MiG-21, the initial-production MiG-21F variant presented a very simple appearance. Key features are the slim and well-tapered nose whose inlet centre-body contained no radar, the undernose pitot boom, the forward-hinged single-piece canopy, the transparency just behind the canopy, the large blade aerial, the slim dorsal spine for wiring and control rods, the relatively small vertical tail, without the later dielectric panel, the brake parachute by the ventral fin, the Fowler flaps with upper-surface track and actuator fairing, and the small blisters for the high-pressure small tyres used in this model.

MiG-21F of the Egyptian air force with canopy open and airbrakes (forward and aft) lowered.

MiG-21PF(SPS) of the Egyptian air force, revealing this variant's modified ventral fin after the removal of the brake parachute to the fairing under the rudder.

Right: MiG-21PFS of the Egyptian air force, displaying the definitive form of vertical tail surface without the dorsal fillet characteristic of the narrow-chord MiG-21F and medium-chord MiG-21PF series.

Below: Looking decidedly operation-weary, this MiG-21 PFS has the intermediate type of vertical tail, with extra chord along the leading edge descending to a small fillet.

This Egyptian air force MiG-21MF is typical of the second-generation 'Fishbed', fully capable of the dual interception and ground-attack roles on the power of the much improved R-13 engine that developed greater power than the R-11 for less weight.

Features developed on the MiG-21 PFMA and carried forward to the MiG-21MF (such as this Egyptian air force example apparently modified with a bulged fairing under the fuselage below the cockpit) were the angle-of-attack sensor on the port side of the nose, the four underwing hardpoints and the removal of the dorsal VHF aerial.

Above: On the runway at its home base of Kuipio-Rissala is a MiG-21bis of the Finnish air force. The long, shallow protruberance under the fuselage between the cockpit and the main landing gear legs is the GSh-23 twin-barrel cannon.

Below: A Soviet air force MiG-21bis is pictured in Finland during a courtesy visit to the USSR's neighbour.

Above: Standard-camouflaged MiG-21 bis fighters of the Finnish air force at rest between sorties at Kuipio-Rissala.

Below: A Soviet MiG-21bis, carrying a pair of 108-Imp gal (490-litre) drop tanks on the outer underwing hardpoints, is seen in natural metal finish, though most Soviet tactical aircraft are camouflaged as a matter of routine.

Above: The nose of the MiG-21 series has grown considerably since the MiG-21F, all models since the MiG-21PF having a larger inlet for greater air intake and location of a centrebody containing radar.

Below: The MiG-21UM is deployed by most air arms with MiG-21 fighters, this being an Egyptian aircraft with unusual blade aerial.

The MiG-21F's pitot boom hinged upwards to prevent damage, and other features were the blade aerial and clear-view dorsal panel.

flaps, which move aft to increase wing area before drooping to increase drag, were hydraulically powered with take-off setting of 24° 30′ and landing setting of 44° 30′. The acuating motor and track fairing were above the tip of each flap. The air trunks feeding the engine ran to each side of the main group of centre-line fuel tanks, seven in number and with capacities of 51.7, 145.2, 13.2, 58.3, 44, 52.8 and 52.8 Imp gal (235, 660, 60, 265, 200, 240 and 240 litres). Total internal fuel capacity was increased to 543.33 Imp gal (2,470 litres) by two leading edge tanks each with a capacity of 38.5 Imp gal (175 litres) and two tanks aft of the main landing gear legs each with a capacity of 24.2 Imp gal (110 litres). Of this total, 514.7 Imp gal (2,430 litres) was usable, extra range being conferred by the fitting on a centreline hardpoint of a 108.8-Imp gal (490-litre) drop tank. The landing gear was of tricycle configuration with hydraulic retraction, the main units pivoting 87°. Compressed-air braking was provided on all three wheels, steering being effected by differential braking of the mainwheels.

Such then was the MiG-21 pre-production aircraft, deliveries of which began late in 1958. Service reports about the type were enthusiastic about its portential rather than its actuality, for it was clear that a number of refinements and additional power would be necessary before the MiG-21's true virtues began to be revealed. Pilots were unanimous about the aircraft's excellent handling and manoeuvrability, while ground crew expressed comparable sentiments about ease of maintenance and general reliability of the aircraft and its systems, this latter resulting generally from the basic simplicity of the whole concept.

Progress was dependent primarily on the efforts of the Tumansky engine team, and in the middle of 1959 there became available a slightly improved version of the R-11, this being rated at 12,676-lb (5,750-kg) afterburning thrust. This allowed the introduction of the first true production model, the MiG-21F (*Forsirovanny* or *Forsazh*, meaning 'boosted'), known to NATO as the 'Fishbed-C'. Development was undertaken with a prototype designated E-6T, and the MiG-21F began to enter service in the last quarter of 1959 to general approval from all branches of the operator service. The initial model was the MiG-21F-1 with the uprated engine, but this was soon joined by improved models such as the MiG-21F-13 with a broader-chord fin and improved Sirena radar tail-warning receiver.

Above: The highly streamlined ventral tank of this MiG-21F contained 108 Imp gal (490 litres) of additional fuel, providing a welcome increase in range over that possible on the 515 Imp gal (2,340 litres) of usable internal fuel.

Above: The low thrust of the original R-11F turbojet meant that the MiG-21F was usually operated without external stores, with the possible exception of two K-13A AAMs.

Left: A MiG-21F at low level with flaps and landing gear lowered.

Weight considerations on the MiG-21F meant that the port-side cannon was not usually fitted, its blast trough being faired over.

Despite the introduction of extra power, the Soviets decided to stick to the single-gun internal armament, the extra power thus going towards an increase in performance rather than enhanced offensive capability. Provision was still made for the port cannon, the blast tube merely being faired-over for aerodynamic reasons.

By this time the virtues of the MiG-21 had been revealed for potential export customers. One of the first was India, which received an initial batch of six MiG-21Fs for evaluation on 28 January 1963. Indian pilots were particularly impressed by the Soviet fighter's handling and manoeuvrability, but expressed some disquiet about its lack of range, relatively light armament and over-simple avionics, with features such as radar-ranging in the inlet centrebody but otherwise no radar. At this stage the MiG-21 was seen in terms only of clear-weather interception under strict ground control in Soviet service, which could afford specialized all-weather interceptors in addition to clear-weather aircraft. However, such were the advantages of the aircraft and the favourable terms offered by the USSR, that India in 1962 decided to build the type under licence, together with the engine. A production facility was established by Hingustan Aeronautics Ltd from its Nasik, Koraput and Hyderabad Divisions, the MiG-21F entering production as the Type 74, the principal alteration in comparison with the Soviet version being the reinstatement of the second cannon. Licence production was also initiated in Czechoslovakia, the main distinguishing feature of the Czech model being the deletion of the small transparent panels aft of the main cockpit canopy. A few examples of the MiG-21F were also delivered to China before the political rift between that country and the USSR in 1960; the Chinese decided after the split with the USSR to undertake the phenomenal task of copying the whole MiG-21/R-11 package without a licence from the USSR, using only the aircraft and engines already delivered as patterns. The Chinese aero industry set to work with a will, and production of a version of an aircraft designated J-7 (Jianjiji-7 or Fighter Aircraft No. 7) began at the Xian factory in 1964, R-11 engines beginning to roll off a

A Finnish MiG-21F is seen with a visiting Soviet MiG-23, the air-superiority type that has largely replaced the MiG-21 series in front-line Soviet service. Note the MiG-21F's lowered flaps and ventral airbrake.

production line at Shenyang in 1965. The J-7 entered service in 1965, and some 80 were built before production was temporarily ended in 1966, possibly as a result of technical difficulties.

By the early 1960s service experience with the MiG-21F had thrown up a number of suggestions as to ways in which this rather basic fighter might be improved in performance and capability. The main features of service criticism concerned the type's lack of range, and also its restriction to clear-weather operations for lack of radar. The problems were not insoluble, but the MiG OKB was severely constrained in its approach by the limited power of the R-11, whose development was lagging behind that of the airframe/avionics package. In late 1960, or early 1961, the MiG OKB flew for the first time a prototype designated E-7. Externally this was distinguishable by a considerably less-tapered forward fuselage section, and by an enlarged dorsal spine just aft of the cockpit. The former, which increased the diameter of the inlet from 2 ft 3.16 in (0.69 m) to 2 ft 11.83 in (0.91 m) at the lip, allowed the incorporation of a larger inlet centrebody to accommodate the R1L search and track radar that provided the new variant with a limited all-weather capability. The latter allowed the incorporation of a substantial saddle tank, with a capacity of 83.6 Imp gal (380 litres), raising overall internal capacity to 626.9 Imp gal (2,850 litres). The E-7 soon proved its superiority over the basic MiG-21F series, and was placed in production as the MiG-21PF (*Perekhvatchik*, or 'interceptor', denoting the provision of radar), which was allocated the NATO reporting name 'Fishbed-D'. The R1L radar is known to NATO as 'Spin Scan-A', and is an equipment of limited capability. The antenna has a diameter of about 40.0 cm (15.74 in), and a range of some 19 km (12 miles) has been claimed for the equipment. Nevertheless, the incorporation of R1L marked a radical improvement in the capabilities of the MiG-21 series. Many other features were built into the MiG-21PF including the relocation of the pitot boom to a position above the nose (earlier aircraft having had the boom below the nose), a boundary-layer discharge system with outlets above and below the nose, a revised canopy with reduced wave drag characteristics, the deletion of the rear-view transparencies in the fashion pioneered by the Czech version of the MiG-21F, the elimination of the remaining gun and all provision for inbuilt barrelled weapons, the simplification of the forward airbrakes, the movement of the main VHF blade aerial from a position aft of the cockpit to a point midway along the dorsal spine, the removal of the secondary VHF aerial that previously occupied the midpoint position, and the installation of larger mainwheels. In the MiG-21F these had been 660×200 mm units with a tyre pressure of 147.6 lb /sq in (10.38 kg/cm²), while the wheels of the MiG-21PF were larger and had a pressure of 115 lb/sq in (8.09 kg/cm²), suiting the later fighter to operations from airfields without paved runways. The use of these larger wheels entailed the provision of large blisters above and below the wing for retracted accommodation. Oddly enough, early MiG-21PFs reverted

The MiG-21PF featured a revised nose of larger diameter and with radar in the inlet centrebody. The pitot was also moved.

to the narrow-chord fin of the first MiG-21Fs, but the broader-chord fin was soon introduced.

The MiG-21PF was built in a number of variants, an early type introducing the broader-chord fin and an uprated powerplant, a middle-range type catering for the installation of two rocket-assisted take-off units to the sides of the ventral airbrake, and the MiG-21PF-17 marking the relocation of the braking parachute to a bullet fairing just below the rudder. The previous installation had been fairly clumsy, the opening of the twin doors of the underfuselage parachute bay allowing the streaming of the 'chute, which pulled the cable from an underfuselage channel and stowage in the ventral fin, to which the end of the cable was attached. The revised system allowed clamshell doors to open, so releasing the 'chute and cable. Other modifications added later in the production run (possibly on the MiG-21PF-31 which was introduced in 1964) were a fin increased in chord by about 0.46 m (1 ft 6.1 in) at the leading edge, which now ran straight down into the dorsal spine and so removed the previous fillet, and the provision of a GP-9 cannon pack as an alternative to the 107.8-Imp gal (490-litre) centreline drop tank. This reflected adverse comment by service pilots, who were unanimous in their condemnation of an armament that had been reduced to a mere two K-13A missiles, which were ineffective against anything but aircraft flying straight and level in clear weather directly in front of the firing aircraft. The GP-9 gun pack proved an exceptional system, and housed a twin-barrel GSh-23 23-mm cannon plus its ammunition. The GSh-23 offered a firing rate of more than 3,000 rounds per minute and an effective range of some 1,420 yards (1,300 m), and the trim GP-9 pack had little effect on aircraft performance or agility, much to the approval of service pilots. To enable optimum use of the GP-9 system, late-production MiG-21PFs were fitted with a predictor sight and ranging system. Under the NATO reporting name system, the late-production MiG-21PF with broad-chord fin and GP-9 pack is designated 'Fishbed-E'. The MiG-21PF was produced by HAL for the Indian Air Force with the local designation Type 76.

The provision of larger and softer mainwheel tyres had done much to improve the tactical capabilities of the MiG-21 series, which was now freed from reliance on long paved runways, whose vulnerability to conventional and/or nuclear attack was becoming increasingly apparent in the early 1960s. However, early deployment of the MiG-19PF to semi-prepared and grass runways confirmed that approach and landing speed of the MiG-21PF were too high for safe operations by average Soviet pilots. The solution was already in hand, for at the 1961 Tushino air display there had been revealed the E-7SPS prototype. This featured a version of the R-11 engine with couplings to permit the tapping of large volumes of air from the front of the combustion chamber for SPS (*Sduva Pogranichnovo Sloya*) or boundary-layer flap-blowing. For this SPS system the previous Fowler flaps were replaced by plain flaps of larger area, lacking the tracks of the Fowler flaps but characterized by large mid-span actuator fairings on the undersides of the wings. The use of these blown flaps reduced landing speed by a useful degree. The SPS system was introduced into production-line aircraft with a model designated MiG-21PFS or MiG-21PF(SPS) by the Soviets, though NATO retained the reporting name 'Fishbed-D' for the type. Other features of this model were the progressive introduction of improved R2L 'Spin Scan-B' search-and-track radar, and the improved R-11-FS-300 and R-11-F2S-300 engines with provision for flap-blowing and a maximum rating of 8,598 lb (3,900-kg) dry thrust and 13,668-lb (6,200-kg) after-burning thrust, the F2S model being marked by a number of

Later MiG-21PFs, such as this Czech aircraft, had a broader-chord vertical tail. Note the dorsal fairing over the saddle tank for increased internal fuel capacity.

The MiG-21PF had a revised canopy of lower drag, and more effective forward airbrakes.

detail improvements that did not add to the thrust.

India's next variant was the MiG-21FL (*Forsazh Lokator*, or 'boosted radar') version of the MiG-21PFS. Though modelled on the blown-flap Soviet model, the MiG-21FL was not provided with the SPS system and was powered by the R-11-300 engine. Despite having R2L radar it lacked a number of Soviet-classified avionics systems and had no provision for rocket-assisted take-off. One hundred examples of the MiG-21FL were supplied as knocked-down components, the first of these flying early in 1967 after the launch of the programme in 1966, when the initial crated components arrived by sea in Bombay. India's licence agreement with the USSR called for an increasing proportion of Indian-manufactured items as production of the Type 77 got under way at Nasik and, by the time the 196th and final Type 77 was delivered in 1973, Indian manufacture totalled some three-fifths of the aircraft.

In about 1964 the MiG OKB had flown the first examples of an improved variant, destined for production under the designation MiG-21PFM. The final letter of the designation suffix indicated *Modifikatsirovanny* or 'modified', and the MiG-21PFM may be regarded as the definitive production model of which the MiG-21PFS was an interim type. All the features of the MiG-21PF-31 and MiG-21PFS were standard and, apart from the provision of a substantial dielectric aerial for VHF/UHF at the top of the fin (also used in late-production MiG-21PF and MiG-21PFS aircraft), the main distinguishing feature was a total revision of the canopy and ejector seat system. The original semi-encapsulated system, in which the canopy had remained attached to the ejector seat had been slowed to a moderate speed by its drogue 'chute, being replaced by a conventional canopy and seat. The new canopy hinged to starboard, and there was a separate fixed windscreen with quarterlights; the ejector seat was an improved model with improved safety features. Like earlier models, the MiG-21PFM was also built in Czechoslovakia, but the MiG-21PFM has the distinction of being the last variant to be produced in that country, whose liberalization during the mid-1960s was a cause for considerable concern in Soviet military and political circles. The NATO designation was 'Fishbed-F'.

Some 12 months after the first MiG-21PFM had flown, the MiG OKB introduced another prototype, the E-9 designed to pave the way for the first true dual-role version of the series, the MiG-21PFMA known to NATO as the 'Fishbed-J'. This version differed significantly from earlier models, not so much in its basic airframe or powerplant (the R-11-300 being retained) but in its avionics and external equipment. The 'Spin Scan' search-and-track radar was replaced by the more capable 'Jay Bird' search-and-track radar, which has the same diameter antenna as the 'Spin Scan' series. More significant, however, was the considerable enlargement of the dorsal spine, whose upper line became virtually straight as far aft as the junction with the leading edge of the fin. The extra volume so provided was used for the accommodation of additional avionics systems, whose bulk in turn necessitated a reduction in internal fuel capacity to 571.9 Imp gal (2,600 litres). At the same time the number of underwing hardpoints was increased from two to four, permitting the carriage of a considerably greater offensive load. Typical external loads were four AA-2 'Atoll' or AA-2-2 'Advanced Atoll' air-to-air missiles and a centreline drop

Chief distinguishing features of the MiG-21F are the pitot boom under the sharply tapered nose, and the lateral guns.

tank (replaceable by the GP-9 cannon pack) in the air-to-air role, or in the ground-attack role four 9.45-in (240-mm) S-24 rockets, or four UV-16-57 rocket pods, or two 1,102-lb (500-kg) and two 551-lb (250-kg) bombs under the wings plus the GP-9 cannon pack under the fuselage. The inner two underwing hardpoints were plumbed for fuel tanks, the possibility of carrying three 107–8-Imp gal (490-litre) drop tanks restoring range lost with the reduction in internal fuel. Another underwing store that could be carried was an electronic countermeasures (ECM) pod, this normally being carried instead of a missile in the air-to-air role.

Other improvements introduced in the MiG-21PFMA were a KM-1 zero/zero ejector seat (capable of operation at zero altitude and zero speed) and an angle-of-attack indicator in a fairing on the port side of the nose; later in the production run, an internal GSh-23 installation was introduced between the forward airbrakes, the ejection chutes for the spent cartridge cases being angled outwards to clear the centreline store, almost always a drop tank once an internal cannon armament had been provided. This later-production model also introduced compatibility with the radar-homing version of the 'Atoll' air-to-air missile.

The export version of the MiG-21PFMA was designated MiG-21M, and was of the type with the internal GSh-23 cannon. This variant was selected for production in India as the Type 96, and the first example was delivered to the Indian Air Force in February 1973.

The MiG-21PFMA was also developed into a specialist tactical reconnaissance aircraft, the MiG-21R, known to NATO as the 'Fishbed-H'. This was produced in several variants, the earliest model having an internal arrangement of cameras in place of the GSh-23 installation, the lower edge of the camera box projecting below the bottom of the fuselage. More common was a version with provision for interchangeable centreline pods carried on the hardpoint normally associated with a drop tank. These pods can accommodate forward-facing and oblique cameras or infra-red linescan equipment, plus fuel. All these MiG-21R variants can carry additional sensor pods under the wings, and have a suppressed antenna on the dorsal spine just forward of the junction with the leading edge of the fin. Partway through MiG-21R production, ECM pods were added at the wingtips.

The tactical flexibility of the MiG-21PFMA and MiG-21R was much appreciated by the Soviet air force and other operators, but not so popular was the considerable worsening of the type's basic power-to-weight ratio, the result of increased external loads without a commensurate increase in power from the R-11 engine, which had reached the end of its development potential. The MiG OKB thus had no alternative but to look at another powerplant if continued development of the basic MiG-21 was to be continued.

Above: The MiG-21PFM was modelled on the late-production MiG-21PF but fitted with a further-broadened vertical tail, blown flaps and a revised cockpit with different ejector seat and side-hinged canopy.

Below: The MiG-21MF was introduced in 1967 and was powered by the R-13 engine of higher mass flow. Note the side-hinged canopy, three drop tanks and large VHF/UHF dielectric panel at the top of the fin.

Above: The instrument fit of all MiG-21s has been generally simple, as indicated by this poor-quality shot of a MiG-21PF's cockpit, dominated by the hooded screen for the R1L search-and-track radar above the artificial horizon.

Second-generation fighter

With the maximum take-off weight of first generation MiG-21 variants moving steadily upwards as extra ordnance and avionics were demanded, performance was eroded as the limits of R-11 engine development were reached. The solution demanded by the MiG OKB, and found by Tumansky, was a revised engine designated R-13. Based on the R-11 series, the R-13 has the same overall dimensions as its predecessor, but is apparently lighter thanks to the provision of a new compressor able to handle a greater airflow than the compressor of the R-11. The R-13 also has a more advanced afterburner, the result being a single-shaft two-spool turbojet with a considerably better power-to-weight ratio than the R-11. Weight saving comes in part from clever design, but also from the use of a large proportion of titanium in the engine, and the R-13 has basic ratings of 11,244-lb (5,100-kg) dry thrust and 14,550-lb (6,600-kg) afterburning thrust. As overall dimensions remained essentially unaltered, it was a relatively simple matter for the MiG OKB to introduce this more powerful engine into what became a second-generation of advanced fighters.

Design work thus began on the revised fighter, designated MiG-21MF by the Soviets and known to NATO, like the MiG-21PFMA, as the 'Fishbed-J'. The first MiG-21MF was apparently flown in 1967 and the type began to enter service with the Soviet air force in 1969 or early 1970. The standard powerplant is the R-13-300, whose extra airflow in comparison with that of the R-11 series demanded the addition of debris guards (small deflector plates) under the auxiliary inlets (suck-in relief doors) by the leading edge of the wing roots. The only other external change was the production-line installation of a nearly faired rear-view mirror above the forward portion of the hinged canopy. This feature was rapidly introduced on several older variants as a retrofit, and is thus not an infallible method of distinguishing the MiG-21MF.

Internally the structure of the wings was considerably refined

The MiG-21MF featured a rear-view mirror in the canopy, an inbuilt 23-mm twin-barrel cannon and debris guards for the suck-in doors.

Right: Clearly visible in this photograph of a MiG-21MF are the blisters in the fuselage sides above the wing roots to accommodate the larger tyres fitted from the MiG-21PF onwards. Also evident is the saddle fairing along the dorsal spine.

Below: From the MiG-21PF-17 onwards the brake parachute was shifted to a bullet fairing at the base of the rudder, as can be seen on this MiG-21MF whose port suck-in auxiliary inlet (just forward of and very slightly below the leading edge of the wing root) is slightly open. Note also the absence of any dorsal antennae.

Left: Visible on the port side of this MiG-21MF's nose is the angle-of-attack sensor fairing introduced on the MiG-21PFMA. Also well displayed is the boundary-layer discharge duct above the nose (the undernose equivalent being less visible just forward of the port door for the nosewheel unit). Note also the debris guard for the suck-in auxiliary inlet, easily seen behind the cockpit-access ladder.

Below: Despite its size, the dorsal fairing of this MiG-21MF does not betoken increased fuel capacity compared with earlier models, for additional electronics in models from the MiG-21PFMA onwards had enforced a reduction to 572 Imp gal (2,600 litres), in part compensated by the ability to uplift three drop tanks.

Above: A MiG-21MF under tow on the perimeter track of a Finnish airfield during a courtesy visit.

Below: The inlet centrebody of the MiG-21MF houses the antenna for the 'Jay Bird' search-and-track radar.

Above: An auxiliary power lead is plugged into a MiG-21MF.

Below: The MiG-21MF presents a clean though somewhat 'blocky' appearance.

and strengthened, the effect being a useful increase in low-level speed. Whereas earlier MiG-21 variants had been limited by structural factors to high subsonic speeds 'on the deck', the MiG-21MF can achieve some 808 mph (1,300 km/h) or Mach 1.06 at sea level. The improved performance of the MiG-21MF in comparison with the MiG-21PFMA persuaded the Indian authorities to curtail production of the MiG-21M/Type 96 in favour of the MiG-21MF, whose Indian designation has yet to be revealed. Production of the MiG-21MF ended in 1981 after the production of a combined MiG-21M/MiG-21MF total of 150 aircraft.

Produced in parallel with the dual-role MiG-21MF was the MiG-21RF tactical reconnaissance model. This carries the same types of reconnaissance equipment as the earlier MiG-21R and, like its predecessor, is designated 'Fishbed-H' by NATO, despite the considerably improved low-altitude performance of this MiG-21MF variant.

Further refinement of the MiG-21MF resulted in the MiG-21SMT, dubbed 'Fishbed-K' by NATO. This was differentiated from the MiG-21MF by a much enlarged dorsal fairing extending as far aft as the brake parachute housing. Though a slightly bulged contour had been given to the dorsal fairing just aft of the cockpit of the MiG-21PF by the installation of a small saddle tank, further enlargement of the MiG-21 series' dorsal spine had resulted from aerodynamic and equipment accommodation requirements, the bulged fairing providing extra internal volume while also reducing drag by an appreciable degree. This tendency was taken to its logical limit in the MiG-21SMT, though the additional volume bestowed by the continued increase in the fairing's size was combined with a rearrangement of avionics items to permit a useful addition to internal fuel capacity of some 66 Imp gal (300 litres). Though performance and stores capability remain basically unaltered in comparison with those of the MiG-21MF, endurance with a single drop tank on the fuselage centreline is increased to 3 hours 30 minutes. The MiG-21SMT can also carry at its wingtips the detachable ECM pods pioneered by the MiG-21R and MiG-21RF tactical reconnaissance aircraft.

Third-generation fighter

As the MiG-21SMT was entering service in about 1971, the MiG OKB was flying the prototype of a third-generation fighter in the MiG-21 series, namely the MiG-21bis, which received the reporting name 'Fishbed-L' when the type was revealed to the West. This new fighter capitalized on all the aerodynamic and equipment advances of its predecessors, but was completely re-engineered structurally to the latest standards, and was provided with more advanced avionics reflecting the technological strides taken by the USSR during the 1960s as a result of its own efforts and an intensive espionage and covert purchase programme. The engine used in the MiG-21bis is the tried and tested R-13-300, but extra range is bestowed by an increase in internal fuel capacity to 637.9 Imp gal (2,900 litres). There are still seven self-sealing tanks in the fuselage as in the original MiG-21s, but the re-engineering of the structure has not only lightened and stiffened the airframe but also made possible an increase in fuel-tank capacity by the introduction of integral tanks. Apart from increased volume for fuel and avionics, the revised structure of the MiG-21bis caters for a considerably longer fatigue life than had been envisaged in earlier variants.

In about 1975 there appeared the ultimate dual-role fighter development of the MiG-21 series, namely the MiG-21bisF, named 'Fishbed-N' by NATO. In structure and avionics there is little difference between the MiG-21bis and MiG-21bisF, though the latter has a standard the two-axis instrument boom first seen on the MiG-21PFMA and designed to provide the pilot with optimum attitude information for the accurate aiming and delivery of air-to-surface weapons. The major change in the MiG-21bisF was thus the introduction of the third engine to be used in the series, the Tumansky R-25. This has the same dimensions and attachment points as the R-13 type, so the installation of this considerably more powerful engine presented no problems for the designers, particularly as the structural strengthening of the MiG-21bis had been undertaken partially with this engine in mind.

Whereas the R-13 had been a development of the original R-11, the R-25 was a completely new engine. Though dimensionally identical with the R-13, the more modern design was centred on an advanced compressor operating at a high pressure ratio, offering a very useful combination of high power and low specific fuel consumption. In full afterburner mode, the R-25 is rated at 16,535-lb (7,500-kg) thrust. And, despite the much greater airflow requirements of the R-25 in comparison with the R-13, no change was required to the inlet of the MiG-21bisF.

A MiG-21bis shows off its late-standard external interceptor armament of two AA-2A and two AA-8 air-to-air missiles.

A Finnish air force MiG-21bis shows off the type's lines, together with the four underwing hardpoints.

Although produced initially with the standard armament provision of all later MiG-21 variants (up to four AA-2 missiles and/or bombs and rockets for ground-attack work), the MiG-21bisF has since 1980 been produced with provision for the much more capable AA-8 'Aphid' dogfighting missile. This may have been derived from the AA-2 in much the same way that the modern versions of the AIM-9 Sidewinder produced in the USA have been derived as far more capable versions of the earlier pursuit-course Sidewinders, and at last offers Soviet fighters the possibility of missile engagement during the course of a short-range turning combat.

The MiG-21bisF remains in relatively small-scale production in 1984, and is also built under licence in India by HAL. Indian production started in 1980 and is scheduled to end in 1984, while it is possible that Soviet production may continue for a couple of years after that, despite the fact that the MiG-21 is obsolescent as an air-combat fighter even in its most advanced MiG-21bisF form. However, there remains a valuable export market for the type, and the very numbers (about 1,500 available to the Soviet air forces make the type useful in that service as a dual-capable air-combat and ground-attack fighter. Thus there appears every reason to see the MiG-21 in Soviet service well into the 1990s, and in overseas service until the first decade of the next century. Total production is probably well in excess of 11,000, and the type has served with some 40 air forces. However, the MiG-21 is not now operated by all of these air arms for a variety of reasons, most often a shift in the balance of superpower politics, which finds smaller countries once within the Soviet bloc now more closely allied with the US-dominated Western bloc. Some of these countries, Egypt being a good example, have considerable numbers of MiG-21s in their inventories but cannot now support them with spares from the Soviet bloc. In this instance there are two compatible alternatives: recourse to Chinese support, production of the Xian J-7 having resumed in that country during 1980 to produce models comparable with the MiG-21MF, and recourse to the Western powers for overhaul or replacement of avionics items. Thus Egyptian MiG-21s have been supplemented and serviced by Chinese aircraft and spares, and have also sprouted a number of Western items such as Smiths head-up displays and Ferranti navigation/attack systems. Not only do these keep otherwise unserviceable aircraft in commission, but they contribute significantly to developing the aircraft past the levels attained by the Soviets, who have recently started to provide in-service MiG-21 aircraft with data-link equipment.

Above: The MiG-21bis has increased fuel capacity and an airframe re-engineered for long fatigue life.

Below: Finnish air force personnel take a close look at a visiting Soviet MiG-21bis dual-role fighter.

Above: Like all MiG-21s from the MiG-21PFM onward, the MiG-21bis has a better ejector seat under separate windscreen and canopy.

Below: The fairing under the afterburner cooling inlet covers the tailplane linkage. Farther forward is an engine-cooling inlet.

What, then, of the MiG-21 as a combat aircraft? As noted above, the type has served with some 40 air forces in its time, and a considerable number of these have used their aircraft in combat: striking examples are the Egyptians and Syrians against Israel, and the Egyptians against Pakistan. The type has also been used in a number of smaller wars (or in relatively small numbers in larger wars, the North Vietnamese air force being a good example of the latter variety during the early 1970s against the might of the US Air Force and US Navy), but it is the experience of the Egyptians, Indians and Syrians which is most illuminating. It must be admitted right from the beginning that the serviceability and pilot-training levels of the Arab air forces in the major confrontations with Israel have been second-rate, and these two factors have played perhaps a decisive part in the total eclipse of the Arab air arms by the fighters of the Israel Defence Force/Air Force. In recent years the Syrian air force has improved its standards by an extraordinary degree, but this advance on the one side was countered on the other side by the fruits of vast experience and the introduction of modern and superlative warplanes such as the McDonnell Douglas F-15 Eagle air-superiority fighter and the General Dynamics F-16 Fighting Falcon air-combat fighter. In the air fighting over the Israeli advance in the Lebanon during 1982, the Syrians committed their best and most experienced air units, many of them flying the MiG-21, and suffered catastrophic losses without inflicting more than the slightest damage on the IDF/AF. The lesson is clear: Soviet aircraft such as the MiG-21, even in their latest variants, are no match even when flown by experienced and skilled pilots, when the opposition comprises yet more skilled pilots with a heritage of success and flying the world's most advanced combat aircraft.

Against less sophisticated opposition, however, the MiG-21 can still give a good account of itself, and pilots of the Indian air force are comparatively well pleased with their MiG-21s. On the debit side they are forced to admit that range is still disastrously short, armament little more than adequate and equipment standards considerably inferior to those of Western air craft of the same generation. The main equipment shortfalls are concerned with the radar and weapons system. Even with the most advanced 'Jay Bird' radar, for example, pilots cannot acquire a 10.97-sq ft (1.0-m^2) target at ranges greater than 20 miles (32 km), whereas Western radars have considerably better lock-on ranges against smaller targets and the 'Jay Bird' equip-

Above the rudder are the radar warning receiver and triple IFF antennae.

Above: Well displayed on this Finnish MiG-21bis is the clamshell-doored housing for the brake parachute under the rudder.

Below: MiG-21bis fighters of the Finnish air force line up opposite the MiG-23s of their Soviet visitors.

ment has no look-down capability whatsoever. Although the inbuilt cannon armament of later variants is considered good by operators of these later models, the missile armament is next to useless. It is interesting to note in this context that Egypt, for example, is making provision for Western missiles (Matra 550 Magic) on its MiG-21s, as it is considered these will improve the combat efficiency of the aircraft to a marked degree.

What of the aircraft itself as a platform for air operations? The answer to this remains most problematical, for while a number of limitations have to be borne in mind, the lesson of the MiG-19's renaissance must not be forgotten. By the mid-1960s this aircraft had been condemned as wholly obsolescent, yet it then emerged as a potent air-combat fighter, its light wing loading and relatively high power-to-weight ratio bestowing a manoeuvrability that enabled it to survive and even to prevail against technically more advanced opposition. The MiG-19's basic philosophy was maintained in the MiG-21, which is again relatively lightly loaded when not carrying ground-attack weapons, and possesses a relatively good power-to-weight ratio. With four AA-2s and full fuel, the power-to-weight ratio of the MiG-21bis is 0.7 to 1 without afterburner and 0.95 to 1 with afterburner, this latter figure improving to 1.1 to 1 if only two AA-2s and 50 per cent fuel are carried. In this latter condition, the theoretical climb rate of the MiG-21bis is some 58,000 ft (17,670 m) per minute, not much inferior to that of the F-16A with similar armament and fuel. What cannot be denied, however, is that the similarly loaded F-16A has double the rate of turn at sea level and only 90 per cent of the MiG-21bis' radius of turn.

Operator experience has convinced most observers that the MiG-21 can almost never achieve its advertised ceiling, even zoom-climbs to an altitude over 50,000 ft (15,240 m) being the exception rather than the rule. However, the tendency in recent years has been for combat to take place at lower altitudes, so this failing may not be significant in operational terms. More important are subsonic endurance and agility, and here the MiG-21 begins to suffer, as a result mainly of design factors. Though the fuel capacity and specific fuel consumption of the MiG-21 variants are not dissimilar from those of Western

Starboard details of a MiG-21bis in service with the Finnish air force.

Though obsolescent in superpower terms, the MiG-21bis still offers countries such as Finland good value for money as an effective low-cost dual-role fighter in the interceptor and ground-attack roles.

contemporaries, a basic design defect reduces the MiG-21's usable fuel capacity by one-third. As fuel is burned, the centre of gravity shifts aft, and once two-thirds has been used the rearward shift reaches critical point, rendering the MiG-21 all but uncontrollable, especially at low speeds. This factor reduces the MiG-21bis' effective fuel capacity from 637.9 to 425.3 Imp gal (2,900 to 1,933 litres), resulting in a typical endurance of only 45 minutes in clean condition, the addition of each 107.8 Imp gal (490 litres) carried in the three possible drop tanks promoting this figure by some 15 minutes. The other design feature now giving operators cause for concern is the delta wing, originally schemed against a requirement calling for a fast-climbing interceptor. At medium altitudes, however, the delta wing develops high drag, and any form of turning combat causes the MiG-21 to lose speed rapidly. The problem is exacerbated by the controls being very heavy despite being powered, so that the pilot becomes rapidly tired as he seeks to throw his rapidly-decelerating fighter around the sky. One positive feature is the possible use of the flaps to promote agility in a turning encounter. These can be selected down at low airspeeds, and close automatically and progressively as airspeeds rise to 420 mph (675 km/h).

In short, the MiG-21 has several important failings as an air-combat fighter, but also has some useful features. Given a skilled pilot and the more modern type of dogfighting missile, the MiG-21 can still give a good account of itself. And the type is available in large numbers to the USSR and its Warsaw Pact allies, opening up the possibility of swamping the more advanced NATO air forces by weight of numbers if not degree of capability. Moreover, the MiG-21 is still a useful ground-attack fighter even if its offensive stores are relatively light, so it still has a future in this role even when it is completely outclassed as an air-combat platform.

Two-seaters and record-breakers

Built in very large numbers as a single-seat production aircraft, the basic MiG-21 was also produced in two-seat forms for training purposes, and was also used as the basis for a considerable number of research and record-breaking aircraft.

With large numbers of single-seaters in service and destined for future production, there was clearly scope in the late 1950s for a two-seat conversion trainer model, and this appeared in about 1962 as the MiG-21U. This was given the NATO reporting name 'Mongol', later changed to 'Mongol-A' when improved two-seaters began to appear. At the time it was thought that the MiG-21U was a simple conversion of the MiF-21F, with a second cockpit added aft of the original cockpit by the simple expedient of reducing fuel volume and deleting the cannon armament. Further research has shown, however, that the type was a hybrid, for apart from the different canopies, each of which opened separately by hingeing to starboard, the aircraft combined featured of the MiG-21F and the MiG-21PF, the inlet and narrow-chord fin being characteristic of the former, and the large mainwheels typical of the latter.

This initial conversion trainer soon proved the worth of the type, and development proceeded apace, the MiG-21U-11 introducing a broader-chord fin, Sirena tail-warning receiver and the relocation of the braking parachute to a position below the rudder.

The next major variant to appear was the MiG-21US (known to NATO as the 'Mongol-B'), a two-seat version of the MiG-21PFS and fitted with a flap-blowing system, plain flaps and the R-11FS engine. Another notable feature was the provision in the rear cockpit of retractable periscopes for the instructor, who enjoyed a singularly unadvantageous view forwards and downwards as he was not raised above the pupil.

A MiG-21U early-production conversion trainer of the Finnish air force is towed out before a sortie.

The MiG-21UM is the definitive trainer model, and based on the MiG-21MF.

Service deliveries of the MiG-21MF turned attention to a two-seat version of this improved dual-role model, and there subsequently appeared the MiG-21UM, based on this airframe and powered by the R-13FS. Like the MiG-21US, the MiG-21UM was designated 'Mongol-B' by NATO, but was of considerably greater operational value as it had the four underwing pylons introduced on the single-seater MiG-21PFMA. It should also be noted that all two-seater versions of the MiG-21 feature the two-axis instrument boom introduced on the MiG-21PFMA and standardized on the MiG-21bis series. The MiG-21 two-seaters have never been as effective as their Western counterparts in the operational conversion role, but have met the demands placed upon them by the Soviets. They must therefore be judged as effective aircraft that have made a considerable contribution to the overall success of the MiG-21 as a service type.

The MiG-21 series was also used for a number of record-breaking flights. The E-33, for example, was the designation of MiG-21U aircraft flown to a pair of women's world records which were established in 1965 and remain unbroken in 1984. On 22 May Natalya Prokhovana flew an E-33 to a maximum altitude of 79,842 ft (24,336 m), and on 23 June of the same year Lydia Zaitseva took up her E-33 to secure a record for sustained height in horizontal flight with an altitude of 62,402 ft (19,020 m). The single-seat MiG-21PF was also used for the establishment of a number of women's world records, the aircraft in this role being designated E-76. These four records were set in 1966 and 1967, and also remain unbeaten to the present day. The four marks are a speed of 1,322.71 mph (2,128.7 km/h) over a 62.1-mile (100-km) closed circuit by Evgenia Martova; a speed of 1,281–265 mph (2,062.00 km/h) over a 310.7-mile (500-km) closed circuit by Marina Soloveva; a speed of 806.638 mph (1,298.16 km/h) over a 621-mile (1,000-km) closed circuit by Lydia Zaitseva; and a speed of 559.399 mph (900.267 km/h) over a 1,242.8-mile (2,000-km) closed circuit by Evgenia Martova. The records were set on 18 February 1967, 16 September 1966, 28 March 1967 and 11 October 1966 respectively.

The MiG-21 was also used as the basis for a number of men's world records. The earliest of these records came in 1959, when Lieutenant Colonel Georgi Mossolov secured for the USSR its first world absolute speed record, a figure of 1,483.831 mph (2,388.00 km/h) being recorded on 31 October in an E-66 powered by an R37F afterburning turbojet. This combination is now known to have been a pre-production MiG-21PF-13 with an R-11 engine. Just 11 months later another record was added by Konstantin Kokkinaki, who took the mark for speed in a 62.1-mile (100-km) closed circuit to 1,335.113 mph (2,148.66 km/h), again in an E-66.

In the following year Mossolov added the record for absolute height to his absolute speed record, attaining an altitude of 113,891 ft (34,714 m) in an E-66A. This was essentially the E-66 (MiG-21PF) fitted with a GRD U2 rocket motor under the rear fuselage. This liquid-propellant engine contributed an additional 6,614-lb (3,000-kg) thrust to the 13,228-lb (6,000-kg) thrust provided by the R37F turbojet. The basic E-66 series was also used for the establishment of a series of four women's time-to-height records, the pilot being Svetlana Savitskaia. The variant used for these records was the E-66B, powered according to the Soviets by a PDM afterburning turbojet and two TTPD rockets. The PDM is believed to have been an R-13 turbojet rated at 15,432-lb (7,000-kg) thrust, and each of the two TTPDs was rated at

A disadvantage of the MiG-21 trainer series is the instructor's position, no higher than that of the front-seat pupil.

5,071-lb (2,300-kg) thrust. In the course of her record climb on 15 November 1974, Savitskaia reached a height of 9,843 ft (3,000 m) in 41.2 seconds, a height of 19,685 ft (6,000 m) in 1 minute 0.1 second, a height of 29,528 ft (9,000 m) in 1 minute 21.0 seconds, and a height of 39,370 ft (12,000 m) in 1 minute 59.3 seconds. As with other women's world records set in the MiG-21 series, this multiple record remains unbeaten in 1974.

All these records had been set in aircraft that were little modified from production aircraft apart from the 'tweaking' of the engine and the addition (in the case of the E-66A and E-66B) of rocket power as an external package. In parallel with the basic MiG-21 series, however, the MiG OKB was working on a related type optimized for considerably higher performance. This family retained the basic wing and tail unit combination of the MiG-21, but used a longer fuselage that incorporated a considerable proportion of steel and titanium, especially in the rear portions of the fuselage, to make possible maximum speeds of considerably more than Mach 2. The series began in 1958 with the E-150, which used the propulsion system designed for the MiG I-7K that had first flown in January 1957. This was the ultimate development of the I-3 series, intended to produce an aircraft of about twice the MiG-21's weight and intended for service in the all-weather fighter and tactical fighter-bomber roles. Though the I-3 and its developments were ultimately rejected in favour of the competing Sukhoi design, the research paid handsome dividends in fields such as structure, powerplant installation, aerodynamics and the integration of radar and weapon systems. The I-7K was powered by a Luylka AL-7F afterburning turbojet, and was the fastest jet-powered delta of its period, with a maximum speed of 1,553 mph (2,500 km/h) or Mach 2.35 at altitude coupled to good ceiling and range figures of 73,820 ft (22,500 m) and 1,118 miles (1,800 km) respectively. The only change made when the I-7K's propulsion system was adopted for the E-150 was the substitution of a Tumansky turbojet for the Lyulka unit, which was proving to have an extraordinarily high specific fuel consumption. The Tumansky engine was not only more economical of fuel, but was shorter and lighter than the previous engine. Apart from this basic change, the complete propulsion system was retained from the inlet to the variable nozzle. The armament was restricted to a pair of K-8 or K-9 air-to-air missiles, and the associated radar (whose designation remains a mystery) was linked to the autopilot to provide automatic control of the aircraft with the intention of providing an optimum trajectory for the missiles. The R-15 turbojet was rated at 20,943-lb (9,500-kg) afterburning thrust, sufficient to give the E-150 a maximum speed of 1,802 mph (2,900 km/h) or Mach 2.73 at altitude. The basic concept was developed with the E-152 prototype of 1959, which introduced a refined avionics system to make the E-152 the USSR's first true all-weather combat aircraft. It may be assumed that these prototypes exhibited a number of undesirable features, for they were pushing forward the current state of the art, and were not placed in production. Such was the importance of the test data generated by the type, however, that continued development was authorized, resulting in 1959 in the appearance of the E-152A. This was distinguishable from the E-152 largely by its rear fuselage, which was considerably altered to provide for two R-11 engines in place of the single R-15A of the E-152. The final development of the E-150 series was the E-152M (known to NATO as the 'Flipper'), although little of this is known apart from the fact that it led to the E-166 series.

The E-166 was produced to meet exacting requirements in the fields of structure and aerodynamics in a research aircraft capable of more than 1,864 mph (3,000 km/h). So whereas the E-150 series had been a compromise between research and operational requirements, with provision for armament and operational systems, the E-166 was intended right from the outset solely as a research platform. The result was a striking aircraft conceptually allied to the MiG-21 and E-150 series, but featuring refined aerodynamics, advanced structure and a high-augmentation version of the AL-7 turbojet. The fuselage was an almost perfect cylinder with only very slight taper at the inlet and nozzle, and surmounted by a massive dorsal spine fairing the cockpit into the vertical tail but also providing considerable volume for fuel and avionics. The special AL-7 was designated TRD P-166 and rated at 22,046-lb (10,000-kg) dry thrust or 33,069-lb (15,000-kg) afterburning thrust. Keys to the optimum use of this powerful turbojet were a massive inlet with translating centrebody offering four cone angles, an upstream boundary-layer dump system with aft-facing doors above and below the nose, auxiliary suck-in doors well aft along the fuselage (midway between the cockpit and the wing roots), and a convergent/divergent nozzle some 50 per cent larger in diameter than the inlet, to provide optimum performance at speeds in the order of Mach 3. The main wheels had special high-pressure tyres so that the slimmest possible section could be used, but even then the thickness of the wheels meant faired bulges in the wings, which were of particularly low thickness/chord ratio. Fuel virtually filled the dorsal spine and the fin, but even so the prodigious consumption of the Lyulka engine provided for a maximum full-throttle endurance of only 12 minutes, a factor that seriously hampered the research programme.

Even so, the E-166 played an important part in the development of the subsequent MiG-25 'Foxbat' Mach 3 interceptor, and in the process set three world records. The first of these came on 7 October 1961, when Colonel Aleksandr Fedotov took the 62.1-mile (100-km) closed-circuit speed record at 1,491.909 mph (2,401.00 km/h). There followed, on 7 July 1962, a world absolute speed record, Lieutenant Colonel Georgi Mossolov attaining 1,665.893 mph (2,681.00 km/h) over a 9.32/15.53-mile (15/25-km) course. And finally, on 11 September 1962 Piotr Ostapenko raised the world record for sustained height in level flight to 74,377 ft (22,670 m). Thus all three of the MiG OKB's chief test pilots had been involved in this series of classic flights, which nevertheless failed to reveal the true potential of the E-166, whose performance parameters included a maximum speed of 1,864 mph (3,000 km/h) and a ceiling of 82,020 ft (25,000 m).

There can be little doubt that the E-166 represented the ultimate expression of the design pioneered by the MiG-21, and as such had little other than a conceptual relationship to its mass-production contemporary. Far closer to the original series, however, were two developments intended to provide a way of reducing take-off run. The first of these was the E-8 prototype with a powered canard foreplane. This was intended to pave the way for an attack derivative, the MiG-21Sht, whose take-off performance and low-level agility would be much enhanced by a canard configuration. The other development was intended purely for research purposes, and was an experimental V/STOL type known to the Soviets as the MiG-21DPD and to NATO (after the type was revealed at the 1967 Domodefovo air display) as the 'Fishbed-G'. This prototype carried no armament and had its fuselage lenghtened by about 3 ft 3.4 in (1.0 m) aft of the cockpit to provide volume for a pair of lift engines. These were located in the vertical position on the centre of gravity, and were fed through a dorsal door hinged at its rear. The two turbojets exhausted through transverse and controllable louvres directly under the centre of gravity. The main landing gear units were fixed, but the nose leg was retractable to mitigate stability problems.

Finally there was the A-144, or MiG-21 'Analog'. This was associated with the design and development effort for the Tupolev Tu-144, the world's first supersonic transport aircraft. The MiG-21 was selected as a suitable basis for a research aircraft using a scaled-down version of the Tu-144 delta wing, and this MiG-21F variant contributed much to the aerodynamic development of the Tu-144, the 'Analog' often acting as chase aircraft and aerodynamic behaviour check during the flight trials of the Tu-144.

Above: In clean condition the MiG-21bis is still notable for its high rate of climb and considerable manoeuvrability.

Below: Ready for a sortie, this MiG-21bis presents an appearance of some menace even at rest on the runway.

Specifications

Mikoyan-Gurevich MiG-21MF technical description

Wings: all-metal cantilever mid-wing monoplane structure with a TsAGI S-12 series aerofoil section and a clipped-wing delta configuration; sweepback is about 57°; anhedral is −2°; thickness/chord ratio decreases from 5.0 per cent at the root to 4.2 per cent at the tip; each of the two wing panels is a single structure mainly of D16-T duralumin with machined skins that have a maximum thickness of 2.5 mm (0.01 in); these skins are machined but not integrally stiffened; the wing structure is based on one main spar (at 33.3 per cent chord) and three auxiliary spars (each indexed 90° to the fuselage centreline), each having V-95 or VM-65 booms and 30KhGSA joints; control in rolls is effected by two tabless ailerons, which are fully powered hydraulically; the twin flaps are of the plain type, blown by engine bleed air, and are hydraulically powered; there is a single fence on each wing, just forward of the outboard portion of the aileron.
Fuselage: all-metal semi-monocoque structure of circular section; the ram-air inlet is located in the nose, with a three-position translating conical centrebody and boundary-layer control slots above and below the inlet trunking; aft of the inlet are, respectively, an avionics bay, the nosewheel retraction bay, the cockpit, fuel tanks, the main landing gear retraction bays (with fuselage blisters to accommodate the wheels after they have swung through 87°), and the support structure for the engine and its afterburner unit; there are two door-type air brakes, located one to each side of the underfuselage, below the wing root leading edges, and one door-type air brake just forward of the ventral fin; all these air brakes are hinged at their forward edges and actuated hydraulically; extending from the cockpit to the base of the fin is a broad dorsal fairing, which accommodates avionics and control rods; offset to starboard above the nose is the pitot static boom, with pitch and yaw vanes, and to starboard of the cockpit is the dynamic pressure probe for the q-feel system; at extreme tail is braking parachute housing.
Tail unit: all-metal cantilever unit; conventional swept fin with hydraulically-powered rudder; on each side of the fuselage are the halves of the single-piece all-moving tailplane, which have anti-flutter weights at their tips; the tailplane is hydraulically powered, there being two ratios selected automatically by a system interconnected with the altimeter and air-speed indicator; tailplane trim is controlled by a buttom on the control column; there is a single large ventral fin.
Landing gear: fully-retractable tricycle type, actuated hydraulically and with a single wheel on each leg; the nosewheel is a castoring unit with pneumatic braking, and retracts forwards; the main units retract inward, and steering is effected by differential use of the pneumatically-operated mainwheel brakes; all landing gear legs have oleo-pneumatic shock-absorption.
Powerplant: one Tumansky R-13-300 turbojet rated at 11,243-lb (5,100-kg) dry thrust and 14,550-lb (6,600-kg) afterburning thrust; this is installed in the rear fuselage on rails which allow the engine to be slipped out to the rear for maintenance and change; air for the engine is drawn through a ram nose inlet with a three-position conical translating centrebody, effective use of this inlet and the long inlet trunking through the forward and centre fuselage being achieved by the use of boundary-layer slots above and below the inlet, and by the provision of suction-relief doors (one on each side of the fuselage) just forward and below the wing root leading edges; maximum power is obtained by use of the afterburner and variable convergent nozzle; internal fuel capacity (all within the fuselage) is 572 Imp gal (2,600 litres), of which only some 396 Imp gal (1,800 litres) is usable as a result of centre-of-gravity movement constraints; external fuel can be carried, the underfuselage hardpoint being able to accept one 108-Imp gal (490-litre) drop tank, and each of the two outer underwing hardpoints being plumbed for a similar 108-Imp gal (490-litre) drop tank; take-off can be shortened by the use of RATO (rocket-assisted take-off) gear, consisting of two jettisonable solid-propellant rockets attached to the underside of the fuselage aft of the mainwheel doors.
Accommodation: pilot only on a KM-1 zero/zero ejector seat in a heated, pressurized and air-conditioned cockpit; the pilot is seated under a canopy that hinges open to starboard, the fixed portion in front of him having quarterlights and a flat bullet-proof windscreen; there is armour protection in front of and behind the cockpit.
Systems: pitch and roll autostabilization system; twin hydraulic systems driven by an engine pump, emergency power being provided by a battery-operated electric pump; the controls are fully powered, with manual control for emergencies, tailplane trim being effected electrically.
Electronics: the principal electronic aid is the 'Jay Bird' search-and-track radar, located in the inlet centrebody; other standard equipment comprises a tail-warning radar receiver (marked in 45° segments to port and starboard forward and behind the aircraft), VOR/ADF ranging and direction-finding navigation equipment, UHF/VHF communications, full blind-flying instrumentation with attitude and heading indicators operated by the central gyro system, and a gyro gunsight.
Armament: inbuilt armament comprises a belly-mounted GSh-23 23-mm twin-barrel cannon with 200 rounds, and the disposable armament is carried on four underwing hardpoints able to carry a maximum load of some 3,307 lb (1,500 kg); in the interception role, armament can comprise two AA-2 'Atoll' (K-13A) and two AA-2-2 'Advanced Atoll' air-to-air missiles, or four AA-2 'Atoll' missiles, or two AA-2 'Atoll' missiles and two drop tanks; ground-attack loads can comprise four UV-16-57 rocket pods, or four S-24 9.45-in (240-mm) unguided rockets, or two 1,102-lb (500-kg) and two 551-lb (250-kg) bombs.

MiG-21PFM

Type:	single-seat limited all-weather interceptor fighter
Accommodation:	pilot only, seated on an ejector seat
Armament:	one GP-9 pack with one GSh-23 23-mm twin-barrel cannon and 200 rounds, plus two underwing hardpoints each able to carry one K-13A (AA-2 'Atoll') air-to-air missile, or one UV-16-57 rocket pod, or one 551-lb (250-kg) bomb, or one 9.45-in (240-mm) rocket
Powerplant:	one Tumansky R-11F2S-300 turbojet rated at 13,668-lb (6,200-kg) afterburning thrust
Performance:	
maximum speed	1,320 mph (2,125 km/h) or Mach 2 at altitude
cruising speed	—
initial climb rate	slightly more than that of MiG-21PF
service ceiling	57,415 ft (17,500 m)
range	comparable with that of the MiG-21PFS
Weights:	
empty equipped	—
normal take-off	-
maximum take-off	about 20,503 lb (9,300 kg)
Dimensions:	
span	23 ft 5½ in (7.15 m)
length	51 ft 8½ in (15.76 m) with probe and about 45 ft 11 in (14.00 m) without probe
height	13 ft 5⅖ in (4.10 m)
wing area	247.6 sq ft (23.00 m^2)

MiG-21PF

Type:	single-seat limited all-weather interceptor fighter
Accommodation:	pilot only, seated in a semi-encapsulated escape system (ejector seat and windscreen)
Armament:	one NR-30 30-mm cannon with ? rounds or (late production) one GP-9 pack with one two-barrel GSh-23 23-mm cannon with 200 rounds, plus two underwing hardpoints each able to carry one K-13A (AA-2 'Atoll') air-to-air missile, or one UV-16-57 rocket pod, or one 551-lb (250-kg) bomb, or one 9.45-in (240-mm) rocket
Powerplant:	one Tumansky R-11F2 turbojet rated at 9,502-lb (4,310-kg) dry thrust and 13,117-lb (5,950-kg) afterburning thrust
Performance:	
maximum speed	1,320 mph (2,125 km/h) or Mach 2 at altitude
cruising speed	—
initial climb rate	slightly better than that of MiG-21F
service ceiling	57,415 ft (17,500 m)
range	slightly more than that of MiG-21F
Weights:	
empty equipped	—
normal take-off	—
maximum take-off	about 20,503 lb (9,300 kg)
Dimensions:	
span	23 ft 5½ in (7.15 m)
length	51 ft 8½ in (15.76 m) with probe and about 45 ft 11 in (14.00 m) without probe
height	13 ft 5⅖ in (4.10 m)
wing area	247.6 sq ft (23.00 m^2)

MiG-21F

Type:	single-seat clear-weather interceptor fighter
Accommodation:	pilot only, seated in a semi-encapsulated escape system (ejector seat and windscreen)
Armament:	one NR-30 30-mm cannon with ? rounds, plus two underwing hardpoints each able to carry one K-13A (AA-2 'Atoll') air-to-air missile, or one UV-16-57 rocket pod, or one 551-lb (250-kg) bomb, or one 9.45-in (240-mm) rocket
Powerplant:	one Tumansky R-11F turbojet rated at 9,502-lb (4,310-kg) dry thrust and 12,676-lb (5,750-kg) afterburning thrust
Performance:	
maximum speed	1,320 mph (2,125 km/h) or Mach 2 at altitude
cruising speed	—
initial climb rate	25,920 ft (7,900 m) per minute
service ceiling	57,415 ft (17,500 m)
range	1,038 miles (1,670 km) with maximum fuel at economical cruising speed at 36,090 ft (11,000 m)
Weights:	
empty equipped	10,797 lb (4,980 kg)
normal take-off	16,248 lb (7,370 kg)
maximum take-off	19,026 lb (8,630 kg)
Dimensions:	
span	23 ft 5½ in (7.15 m)
length	51 ft 8½ in (15.76 m) with probe and 44 ft 2 in (13.46 m) without probe
height	13 ft 5⅖ in (4.10 m)
wing area	247.6 sq ft (23.00 m^2)

MiG-21MF

Type:	single-seat limited all-weather interceptor and ground-attack fighter
Accommodation:	pilot only, seated on a KM-1 zero/zero ejector seat
Armament:	one GSh-23 23-mm twin-barrel cannon with 200 rounds plus four underwing hardpoints able to carry a total load of 3,307 lb (1,500 kg) including K-13A (AA-2 'Atoll') and AA2-2 'Advanced Atoll' air-to-air missiles, UV-16-57 rocket pods, 551-lb (250-kg) bombs and 9.45-in (240-mm) rockets
Powerplant:	one Tumansky R-13-300 turbojet rated at 11,243-lb (5,100-kg) dry thrust and 14,550 lb (6,600 kg) afterburning thrust
Performance:	
maximum speed	1,385 mph (2,230 km/h) or Mach 2.1 at altitude
cruising speed	—
initial climb rate	36,090 ft (11,000 m) per minute
service ceiling	57,415 ft (17,500 m)
range	230-mile (370-km) hi-lo-hi radius with four bombs, or 683 miles (1,100 km) clean on internal fuel, or 1,118 miles (1,800 km) for ferrying
Weights:	
empty equipped	—
normal take-off	18,078 lb (8,200 kg) with two AAMs
maximum take-off	20,723 lb (9,400 kg)
Dimensions:	
span	23 ft 5½ in (7.15 m)
length	51 ft 8½ in (15.76 m) with probe and about 45 ft 11 in (14.00 m) without probe
height	13 ft 9⅖ in (4.50 m)
wing area	247.6 sq ft (23.00 m^2)

MiG-21PFS

Type:	single-seat limited all-weather interceptor fighter
Accommodation:	pilot only, seated in a semi-encapsulated escape system (ejector seat and windscreen)
Armament:	one GP-9 pack with one GSh-23 23-mm twin barrel cannon and 200 rounds, plus two underwing hardpoints each able to carry one K-13A (AA-2 'Atoll') air-to-air missile, or one UV-16-57 rocket pod, or one 551-lb (250-kg) bomb, or one 9.45-in (240-mm) rocket
Powerplant:	one Tumansky R-11F2S turbojet rated at 9,502-lb (4,310-kg) dry thrust and 13,117-lb (5,950-kg) afterburning thrust
Performance:	
maximum speed	1,320 mph (2,125 km/h) or Mach 2 at altitude
cruising speed	—
initial climb rate	similar to that of the MiG-21PF
service ceiling	57,415 ft (17,500 m)
range	comparable with that of the MiG-21PF
Weights:	
empty equipped	—
normal take-off	—
maximum take-off	about 20,503 lb (9,300 kg)
Dimensions:	
span	23 ft 5½ in (7.15 m)
length	51 ft 8½ in (15.76 m) with probe and about 45 ft 11 in (14.00 m) without probe
height	13 ft 5⅖ in (4.10 m)
wing area	247.6 sq ft (23.00 m^2)

MiG-21PFMA

Type:	single-seat limited all-weather interceptor and ground-attack fighter
Accommodation:	pilot only, seated on a KM-1 zero/zero ejector seat
Armament:	one GSh-23 23-mm twin-barrel cannon with 200 rounds (carried externally in a GP-9 pack on early aircraft and internally on late aircraft), plus four underwing hardpoints able to carry a total load of 3,307 lb (1,500 kg) including K-13A (AA-2 'Atoll') air-to-air missiles, UV-16-57 rocket pods, 551-lb (250-kg) bombs and 9.45-in (240-mm) rockets
Powerplant:	one Tumansky R-11F2S-300 turbojet rated at 13,668-lb (6,200-kg) afterburning thrust
Performance:	
maximum speed	1,320 mph (2,125 km/h) or Mach 2 at altitude
cruising speed	—
initial climb rate	comparable with that of MiG-21PFM
service ceiling	57,415 ft (17,500 m)
range	comparable with that of the MiG-21PFM
Weights:	
empty equipped	—
normal take-off	—
maximum take-off	—
Dimensions:	
span	23 ft 5½ in (7.15 m)
length	51 ft 8½ in (15.76 m) with probe and about 45 ft 11 in (14.00 m) without probe
height	13 ft 5⅖ in (4.10 m)
wing area	247.6 sq ft (23.00 m^2)

MiG-21SMT

Type:	single-seat limited all-weather interceptor and ground-attack fighter
Accommodation:	pilot only, seated on a KM-1 zero/zero ejector sea
Armament:	one GSh-23 23-mm twin barrel cannon with 200 rounds, plus four underwing hardpoints able to carry a total load of 3,307 lb (1,500 kg) including AA-2 'Atoll' (K-13A) or AA-2-2 'Advanced Atoll' air-to-air missiles, UV-16-57 rocket pods, 551-lb (250-kg) bombs and 9.45-in (240-mm) rockets
Powerplant:	one Tumansky R-13-300 turbojet rated at 11,243-lb (5,100-kg) dry thrust and 14,550-lb (6,600-kg) afterburning thrust
Performance:	
maximum speed	1,385 mph (2,230 km/h) or Mach 2.1 at altitude
cruising speed	—
initial climb rate	-
service ceiling	57,415 ft (17,500 m)
range	marginally better than that of MiG-21MF
Weights:	
empty equipped	—
normal take-off	-
maximum take-off	—
Dimensions:	
span	23 ft 5½ in (7.15 m)
length	51 ft 8½ in (15.76 m) with probe and about 45 ft 11 in (14.00 m) without probe
height	13 ft 9⅖ in (4.50 m)
wing area	247.6 sq ft (23.00 m^2)

E-2A

Type: single-seat interceptor fighter development aircraft

Accommodation: pilot only, seated in a semi-encapsulated escape system (ejector seat and windscreen)

Armament: three NR-30 30-mm cannon

Powerplant: one Tumansky RD-9E turbojet rated at 11,243-lb (5,100-kg) afterburning thrust

Performance:

maximum speed	1,205 mph (1,940 km/h) or Mach 1.82 at altitude
cruising speed	—
initial climb rate	—
service ceiling	—
range	—

Weights:

empty equipped	—
normal take-off	—
maximum take-off	—

Dimensions:

span	—
length	—
height	—
wing area	—

MiG-21/E-6

Type: single-seat clear-weather interceptor fighter development aircraft

Accommodation: pilot only, seated in a semi-encapsulated escape system (ejector seat and windscreen)

Armament: two NR-30 cannon with ? rounds per gun

Powerplant: one Tumansky R-11 turbojet rated at 8,598-lb (3,900-kg) dry thrust and 11,243-lb (5,100-kg) afterburning thrust

Performance:

maximum speed	1,320 mph (2,125 km/h) or Mach 2 at altitude
cruising speed	—
initial climb rate	—
service ceiling	—
range	—

Weights:

empty equipped	—
normal take-off	—
maximum take-off	—

Dimensions:

span	23 ft 5½ in (7.15 m)
length	51 ft 8½ in (15.76 m) with probe and about 44 ft 2 in (13.46 m) without probe
height	13 ft 5⅖ in (4.10 m)
wing area	247.6 sq ft (23.00 m^2)

E-152A

Type: single-seat advanced interceptor development aircraft

Accommodation: pilot only, seated on an ejector seat

Armament: two K-8 or K-9 air-to-air missiles carried on underwing hardpoints

Powerplant: two Tumansky R-11F turbojets, each rated at 9,502-lb (4,310-kg) dry thrust and 12,676-lb (5,750-kg) afterburning thrust

Performance:

maximum speed	1,553 mph (2,500 km/h) or Mach 2.35 at altitude
cruising speed	—
initial climb rate	—
service ceiling	68,900 ft (21,000 m)
range	1,429 miles (2,300 km)

Weights:

empty equipped	—
normal take-off	31,305 lb (14,200 kg)
maximum take-off	—

Dimensions:

span	29 ft 5⅛ in (8.97 m)
length	64 ft 11½ in (19.80 m)
height	—
wing area	303.55 sq ft (28.20 m^2)

MiG-21bis

Type: single-seat limited all-weather interceptor and ground-attack fighter

Accommodation: pilot only, seated on a KM-1 zero/zero ejector seat

Armament: one GSh-23 23-mm twin-barrel cannon with 200 rounds, plus four underwing hardpoints able to carry a total load of 3,307 lb (1,500 kg) including AA-2 'Atoll' (K-13A), AA-2-2 'Advanced Atoll' and AA-8 'Aphid' air-to-air missiles, UV-16-57 rocket pods, 1,102-lb (500-kg) and 551-lb (250-kg) bombs, and 9.45-in (240-mm) rockets

Powerplant: one Tumansky R-13-300 turbojet rated at 11,243-lb (5,100-kg) dry thrust and 14,550 lb (6,600-kg) afterburning thrust; from 1975 fitted with Tumansky R-25 (see MiG-21bisF)

Performance:

maximum speed	1,385 mph (2,230 km/h) or Mach 2.1 at altitude
cruising speed	—
initial climb rate	—
service ceiling	57,415 ft (17,500 m)
range	comparable with that of MiG-21SMT

Weights:

empty equipped	—
normal take-off	—
maximum take-off	—

Dimensions:

span	23 ft 5½ in (7.15 m)
length	51 ft 8½ in (15.76 m) with probe and about 45 ft 11 in (14.00 m) without probe
height	13 ft 9⅖ in (4.50 m)
wing area	247.6 sq ft (23.00 m^2)

MiG-21bisF

Type: single-seat limited all-weather interceptor and ground-attack fighter

Accommodation: pilot only, seated on a KM-1 zero/zero ejector seat

Armament: one GSh-23 23-mm twin-barrel cannon with 200 rounds plus four underwing hardpoints able to carry a total load of 3,307 lb (1,500 kg) including AA-2 'Atoll' (K-13A), AA-2-2 'Advanced Atoll' and AA-8 'Aphid' air-to-air missiles, 1,102-lb (500-kg) and 551-lb (250-kg) bombs, UV-16-57 rocket pods, and 9.45-in (240-mm) rockets

Powerplant: one Tumansky R-25 turbojet rated at 12,787-lb (5,800-kg) dry thrust and 16,535 lb (7,500-kg) afterburning thrust

Performance:

maximum speed	1,385 mph (2,230 km/h) or Mach 2.1 at altitude
cruising speed	—
initial climb rate	58,005 ft (17,680 m) per minute with two AAMs and half fuel
service ceiling	57,415 ft (17,500 m)
range	about 720 miles (1,160 km) on internal fuel at high altitude, or 988 miles (1,590 km) with external fuel

Weights:

empty equipped	11,465 lb (5,200 kg)
normal take-off	17,550 lb (7,960 kg)
maximum take-off	22,046 lb (10,000 kg)

Dimensions:

span	23 ft 5½ in (7.15 m)
length	51 ft 8½ in (15.76 m) with probe and about 45 ft 11 in (14.00 m) without probe
height	13 ft 5⅖ in (4.10 m)
wing area	247.6 sq ft (23.00 m^2)

E-166

Type: supersonic development aircraft

Accommodation: pilot only, seated on an ejector seat

Armament: none

Powerplant: one highly-developed Lyulka AL-7F turbojet rated at 22,046-lb (10,000-kg) dry thrust and 33,069-lb (15,000-kg) afterburning thrust

Performance:

maximum speed	1,864 mph (3,000 km/h) or Mach 2.82 at altitude
cruising speed	—
initial climb rate	—
service ceiling	82,020 ft (25,000 m)
range	—

Weights:

empty equipped	about 18,739 lb (8,500 kg)
normal take-off	—
maximum take-off	about 44,092 lb (20,000 kg)

Dimensions:

span	29 ft 5⅛ in (8.97 m)
length	about 59 ft 0⅔ in (18.00 m)
height	—
wing area	about 312.16 sq ft (29.00 m^2)

Acknowledgments

Aviation Photographers International/Anderson: p. 5 (bottom).
Aviation Photographers International/Peacock: p. 4, 5 (top), 8, 9 (top), 10.
Department of Defense: p. 30, 31, 32, 33, 41, 43 (top).
Finnish Air Force: p. 26–27, 42, 53.
Flight International: p. 6–7.
Dennis Hughes: p. 18–21, 24 (bottom).
Novosti Press Agency: p. 29.
Royal Swedish Air Force: p. 43 (bottom).
US Navy Photo: p. 2–3, 15.